BASKETBALL LEGENDS

Kareem Abdul-Jabbar

Charles Barkley

Larry Bird

Wilt Chamberlain

Julius Erving

Patrick Ewing

Anfernee Hardaway

Grant Hill

Magic Johnson

Michael Jordan

Shaquille O'Neal

Scottie Pippen

CHELSEA HOUSE PUBLISHERS

BASKETBALL LEGENDS

MICHAEL JORDAN

Sean Dolan

Introduction by
Chuck Daly

CHELSEA HOUSE PUBLISHERS
New York · Philadelphia

Produced by Daniel Bial Agency
New York, New York.

Picture research by Alan Gottlieb
Cover illustration by Bradford Brown

5 7 9 8 6 4

Dolan, Sean.
    Michael Jordan / Sean Dolan.
        p.   cm. — (Basketball legends)
    Includes bibliographical reference and index.
    IBSN 0-7910-2432-6 (hard) : $14.95
    1. Jordan, Michael, 1963–   —Juvenile literature. 2. Basketball
players—United States—Biography—Juvenile literature.
[1. Jordan, Michael, 1963–   . 2. Basketball players. 3. Afro-
Americans—Biography.] I. Title. II. Series.
GV884.J67D65 1994
796.323'092—dc20
[B]
                                                            94-5579
                                                               CIP
                                                                AC

CONTENTS

BECOMING A
BASKETBALL LEGEND

Chuck Daly

What does it take to be a basketball superstar? Two of the three things it takes are easy to spot. Any great athlete must have excellent skills and tremendous dedication. The third quality needed is much harder to define, or even put in words. Others call it leadership or desire to win, but I'm not sure that explains it fully. This third quality relates to the athlete's thinking process, a certain mentality and work ethic. One can coach athletic skills, and while few superstars need outside influence to help keep them dedicated, it is possible for a coach to offer some well-timed words in order to keep that athlete fully motivated. But a coach can do no more than appeal to a player's will to win; how much that player is then capable of ensuring victory is up to his own internal workings.

In recent times, we have been fortunate to have seen some of the best to play the game. Larry Bird, Magic Johnson, and Michael Jordan had all three components of superstardom in full measure. They brought their teams to numerous championships, and made the players around them better. (They also made their coaches look smart.)

I myself coached a player who belongs in that class, Isiah Thomas, who helped lead the Detroit Pistons to consecutive NBA crowns. Isiah is not tall—he's just over six feet—but he could do whatever he wanted with the ball. And what he wanted to do most was lead and win.

All the players I mentioned above and those whom this

series will chronicle are tremendously gifted athletes, but for the most part, you can't play professional basketball at all unless you have excellent skills. And few players get to stay on their team unless they are willing to dedicate themselves to improving their talents even more, learning about their opponents, and finding a way to join with their teammates and win.

It's that third element that separates the good player from the superstar, the memorable players from the legends of the game. Superstars know when to take over the game. If the situation calls for a defensive stop, the superstars stand up and do it. If the situation calls for a key pass, they make it. And if the situation calls for a big shot, they want the ball. They don't want the ball simply because of their own glory or ego. Instead they know—and their teammates know—that they are the ones who can deliver, regardless of the pressure.

The words "legend" and "superstar" are often tossed around without real meaning. Taking a hard look at some of those who truly can be classified as "legends" can provide insight into the things that brought them to that level. All of them developed their legacy over numerous seasons of play, even if certain games will always stand out in the memories of those who saw them. Those games typically featured amazing feats of all-around play. No matter how great the fans thought the superstars, the players were capable yet of surprising them, their opponents, and occasionally even themselves. The desire to win took over, and with their dedication and athletic skills already in place, they were capable of the most astonishing achievements.

CHUCK DALY, currently the head coach of the New Jersey Nets, guided the Detroit Pistons to two straight NBA championships, in 1989 and 1990. He earned a gold medal as coach of the 1992 U.S. Olympic basketball team—the so-called "Dream Team"—and was inducted into the Pro Basketball Hall of Fame in 1994.

1
DON'T TALK TO MICHAEL

Everyone should have known better. The players, the press, the fans, the viewers on television, *everyone* should have known what was coming. No one should have been surprised. After all, they had all seen it before.

It was June 1993, and the Chicago Bulls, the two-time defending NBA champions, were fighting for their life. They found themselves in the rarest of positions for them, behind in a playoff series—in this case the Eastern Conference Finals, where they trailed the New York Knicks two games to one.

Over the last two seasons, the Knicks had become the Bulls' fiercest rivals. In the previous year's playoffs, New York had unexpectedly extended Chicago to seven games, utilizing a punishing defensive style reminiscent of the Bulls' great nemesis from years past, the Detroit Pistons. In the just concluded regular season, New

Perhaps the greatest defensive player ever, Michael Jordan stuck to John Starks like glue on defense in the 1993 Bulls-Knicks playoffs.

York had actually bested Chicago for the Eastern Conference's best record and had won the season series from the Bulls.

The Knicks entered the series with the Bulls confident that they could dethrone the champions and advance to the NBA Finals themselves. Mouthy, brash, and relentlessly physical, the Knicks infuriated the Bulls like no other team. In particular, three of the youngest Knicks—Anthony Mason, Greg Anthony, and John Starks—had made themselves notorious with their penchant for trash-talking and intimidation.

Chicago's superstar guard Michael found the on-court confidence of the New York trio to be misplaced and infuriating. Mason, Anthony, and Starks, said Jordan before the 1993 playoffs, were "three of the cockiest guys in the league," with no NBA achievements that would justify their running off at the mouth.

But in the first two games of the 1993 finals, New York seemed prepared to justify its cockiness. On its home court, the Knicks defeated the Bulls twice, dominating both games with physical play that gave them a strong advantage in rebounds. Even more surprising was that Starks, a refugee from basketball's minor leagues, had outplayed Jordan, the league's seven-time scoring champion, three-time most valuable player, and all-time most spectacular player. Near the end of game two, Starks had even punctuated his performance with a soaring lefthanded dunk over three Bulls along the right baseline that was so awe-inspiring that only one adjective could do it justice—Jordanesque. Then in game three, Starks had even had the temerity to charge Jordan on the floor and attempt to start a fight.

Though Chicago had won game three, it still trailed in the series, and Jordan, by his exalted standards, had still not played well. The newspapers were full of stories of how Starks had outplayed him, and the flamboyant dunk was replayed on television again and again. One Chicago columnist even suggested that Jordan had lost a step and was nearing the end of his career. The media also suggested that his uncharacteristic play was due to his being in an Atlantic City, New Jersey, casino gambling until the wee hours of the morning on the day of the first game in New York. For the first time in his career, which had always been characterized by an extreme degree of cooperation with the media, Jordan stopped talking to reporters.

The kids in the schoolyards, to whom Jordan was a veritable basketball god, knew what had happened, and it was unthinkable: Michael had been "dissed." Trash-talking had long since become part of the professional game, an accepted means of on-court expression and self-assertiveness, but there was one rule of NBA etiquette that was inviolable: Do not talk to Michael. The unwritten rule was both a tribute to Jordan's unparalleled stature in the game and a means of self-protection for those faced with the most unwelcome task of guarding him. A defender's prospects in that situation were dire at best, but to offend the boundless pride that smoldered within Jordan at all times was to court total ruin and humiliation.

Those who broke the rule and disrespectfully addressed his oncourt majesty invariably paid a fearsome price. The most recent example had taken place during the regular season. A young

During the second game of the playoffs, Jordan's intensity never slackened, even while he was sitting on the bench.

guard for the Washington Bullets named LaBradford Smith enjoyed a particularly good night against Jordan—scoring 35 points—during a less than critical midseason encounter with Chicago in which the Bulls, certain of a victory over the hapless Bullets, were perhaps going through the motions. "Good game," said Smith to Jordan as the players left the court. The outraged Bulls star interpreted the pleasantry as a taunt, and just a couple of nights later, when he was matched up with Smith again, he went off for 39 points—in the first half.

To his teammates, who were the most frequent firsthand witnesses, Jordan's pride was legendary. His fanatical competitiveness made it difficult for him to let up even in practice, and he was so good a player that he often disrupted drills and scrimmages. Each year, Chicago was forced to reserve a spot on its roster for a player who would serve as Jordan's practice fodder—someone with an ego strong enough to withstand the daily humiliation of going against the best one-on-one player in the history of the game and still continue to practice hard, thereby providing Jordan with at least a modicum of competition. These players were always singularly toughminded individuals, said Bulls assistant coach John Bach, guys you would want to share a foxhole with. Yet after practicing each day against Jordan, they invariably ended the season with their confidence shattered and were seldom of any use in the league again.

"During the first drills, that's when I figured out he was so competitive," said Cliff Levingston, who played for the Bulls in 1990-91, their first championship season. "I said to Craig [Hodges, a teammate], 'Is he always like this?' He said,

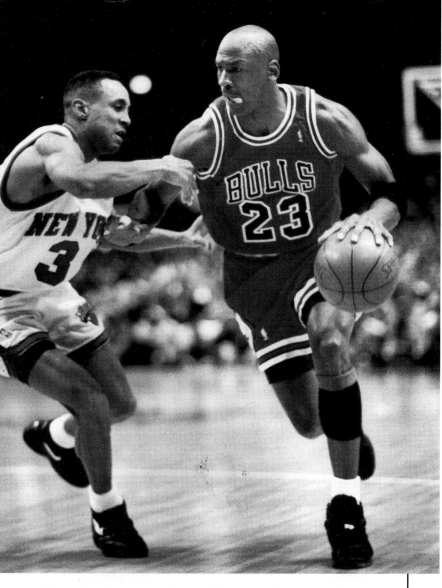

Displaying concentration, drive, and a little tongue, Michael Jordan blew toward the basket past a frustrated John Starks.

'Man, he hates to lose. Hates to lose. And you can't give him anything. Don't let him have his way with you or he will look down on you.'" Witnesses still marveled at the absolute ferocity, replete with some savage trash-talking, with which Jordan had dismembered Adrian Branch several years earlier at a Chicago training camp. Already an established star, Jordan seemingly had nothing to prove in his encounter with Branch, who was then a journeyman struggling just to make the Chicago roster. Years earlier, however, Branch had been one of several nationally acclaimed high-school stars who had treated the less well known Jordan disrespectfully at a time when he was trying to establish his own reputation. The roots of Jordan's pride ran deep.

In the summer before the 1992 season, another set of teammates learned about the perils of disrespecting Michael. Jordan was then a member of the U.S. Olympic basketball team, the so-called Dream Team composed of the best players in the NBA plus one college star. Tired from his second championship season, secure in the abilities of his teammates, and not overly stimulated by the low level of competition, Jordan did not exert himself too greatly at the Olympics. But one day in practice, the Dream Team split into two squads for what would be termed the "greatest pick-up game ever played," and when Magic Johnson's team jumped to a big lead, the former Los Angeles Laker great made the mistake of talking some trash to Jordan.

The result, said those who witnessed it, was breathtaking: Jordan took over the game as easily and completely, on offense and defense, as if the competition were a bunch of out-of-shape stiffs at the local YMCA and not the best players in the world, and his side prevailed. "The one thing I learned at the Olympics," said the team's coach, Chuck Daly, "was that as good as everyone thinks Michael is, he's even that much better."

So no one should really have been too surprised at what occurred after Jordan, a look of grim determination on his face—"he looked," wrote a New York sportswriter, "as if he was on his way to his own execution"—took the floor at Chicago Stadium for game four. The only surprise, really, was the form it took. Taunting the lippy New York guard virtually every time he touched the ball, Jordan torched the helpless Starks for 54 points. Famed for his serpentine, freewheeling drives to the hoop, Jordan on this night took Starks way outside and bombed away, shredding the Knicks' defense, which was the best in the league.

"He was in the zone," a shellshocked Starks said afterwards. "There was nothing I could do." In the next contest, Jordan continued his physical and psychological whipping of the beleaguered Knick guard, tormenting him with insults about his character and game, harassing him into turnovers and poor shooting, scoring 18 consecutive Chicago points himself during a critical stretch of the third and fourth quarters, and passing for an assist on the game's most critical bucket. Chicago won both games and then put the Knicks away in the sixth contest to advance to the finals for the third straight year. "It looked like Michael was doing a lot of talking out there tonight," a reporter said to Starks in the somber Knicks lockerroom after game six. "Did you say anything back to him?" "No," a subdued Starks replied. "I was just trying to keep up with him."

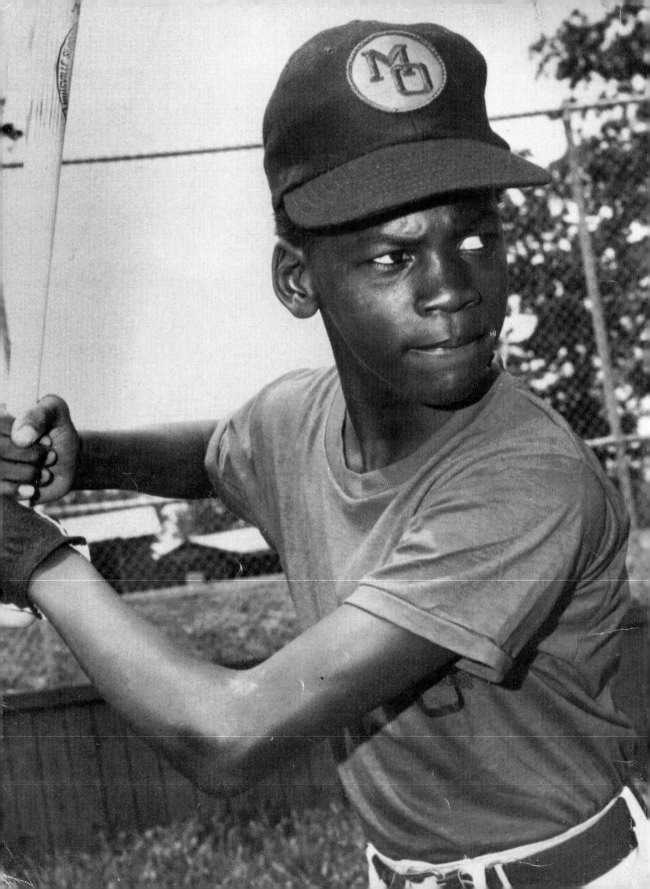

2

WILLFUL
AND LAZY

Michael Jeffrey Jordan was born on February 17, 1963, to James and Deloris Jordan. James Ronald Jordan was their oldest child; he was followed by Deloris, Larry, and then Michael, who was himself followed several years later by Roslyn.

Both of Michael's parents were from small towns in North Carolina. Michael was born in Brooklyn, New York, though, as his father was attending school there in the hope of bettering his position at General Electric. James Jordan worked first as a forklift operator and then as a dispatcher for GE in Wallace, North Carolina.

A couple of months before Michael was born, Deloris Jordan's mother died. The death was unexpected, and the mother and her daughter had been extremely close. Grief and stress nearly caused Deloris to have a miscarriage, and her doctors remained extremely concerned about the health of the baby she was carrying.

Jordan's first love was for baseball. Here he is at age 12, showing good form.

Michael was born with a nosebleed, and the doctors worried that this was a sign that something more serious was wrong. They kept the baby in the hospital for several days after his mother was sent home, but he proved to be in good health, even though he would have nosebleeds for no reason until he was five years old.

Michael's parents often had to worry about his mischievous, daredevil streak. As a two-year-old, he was almost electrocuted in a backyard accident, and at age five he nearly cut off his big toe while playing with an ax.

Attempts to discipline Michael usually proved fruitless, for though he was outgoing and charming, he was also extremely strong willed. "If there was something to be tried," according to Deloris Jordan, "he was the one to try it. If someone needed to be disciplined more, he was the one who needed it. He was going to test you to the end."

In 1970, when Michael was seven, the Jordans moved to Wilmington, a small city by the Atlantic Ocean in southeast North Carolina. "We'd have every kid in the neighborhood at our house in Wilmington because it was the only one with a basketball court," James Jordan recalled. "There would be 20 guys over between the ages of 10 and 18. That's how Michael learned how to play. We were almost like a park. Deloris would buy 15 pounds of hot dogs and hamburgers and we'd make a picnic out of it."

As the smallest and youngest of the backyard competitors, Michael had to learn quickly and play hard if he wanted to take part in the games. The best way for a young basketball player to develop skills is to play against older and better players. A number of past and present NBA greats—Jordan, Larry Bird, Magic Johnson, Isiah Thomas, Scottie Pippen, and Bill Russell, to name just a few—have been younger brothers in athletically-inclined families who learned the game by playing against their older brothers and their friends.

Michael's main competition in his back-yard was his brother Larry, who was one year older and, if the tales can be believed, an even better leaper than his brother. Unfortunately for his own basketball prospects, Larry only grew to 5'8". Even so, for many years, Larry invariably won their hardfought one-on-one contests, which often ended with punches being thrown.

Today, Michael gives Larry a lot of the credit for his hoops development. "Those backyard games really helped me become the player I am in a lot of ways," he says. "Larry would never give me any slack, never took it easy on me. He'd rather beat me up than have me beat him in a game. I learned a lot about being competitive from him."

But for a long time, basketball was not even Michael's favorite sport. Baseball was, and it was as a baseball player that he first attracted attention for his athletic abilities.

"The way he played baseball in Little League, he made me become a fan," his father remembered. "If I wouldn't take him to play ball, he'd look so pitiful, like he'd lost every friend in the world and was all by himself. You'd take one look at him and say 'Okay, let's go.'"

To this day, Michael considers the state baseball championship he won with his Babe Ruth League team to be one of his greatest achievements. "My favorite memory, my great-

In high school, Michael Jordan was called "Bald Head," and he admitted to feeling "goony-looking."

Jordan did not play for his high school varsity team during his sophomore year, as a much taller player beat him out. The next year, after a lot of hard work, Jordan made the team, and had become the best jumper in the area.

est accomplishment," he said in 1991, "was when I got the Most Valuable Player award when my team won the state baseball championship. That was the first thing I accomplished in my life, and you always remember the first. I remember I batted over .500, hit five home runs in seven games, and pitched a one-hitter to get us into the championship game."

Although Michael's athletic abilities thrilled his father, other aspects of his personality did not. James Jordan had grown up poor, and he believed in hard work. But Michael, he said, "was probably the laziest kid I had. He would give every last dime of his allowance to his brothers and sisters and kids in the neighborhood to do his chores for him. . . . That really got me." To James Jordan, who was already working in the tobacco fields on a tractor at age 10, his son's attitude toward work was hard to accept.

Michael's attitude toward hard work changed in his sophomore year at Laney High School in Wilmington. By now, basketball had replaced baseball as Michael's favorite sport. He fully expected to make the varsity basketball team, but Coach Fred Lynch cut him from the squad.

The event shocked him. "I'll never forget how hurt I was," he said years later. "I cried." Michael was so angry that he could not even bring himself to root for the varsity team to win.

He responded by going to work—on his game. Determined to prove the coach wrong, he rose each morning at six to practice and train by himself for hours before school began. He would maintain this regimen for the rest of his time in high school, and as a junior and a senior he became the star of the Laney varsity, averaging more than 20 points a game and first displaying the high-flying, gravity-defying moves that would make him a legend.

"I've got to believe one thing," his father said. "One day, God was sitting around and decided to make Himself the perfect basketball player. He gave him a little hardship early in life to make him appreciate what he would earn in the end, and called him Michael Jordan."

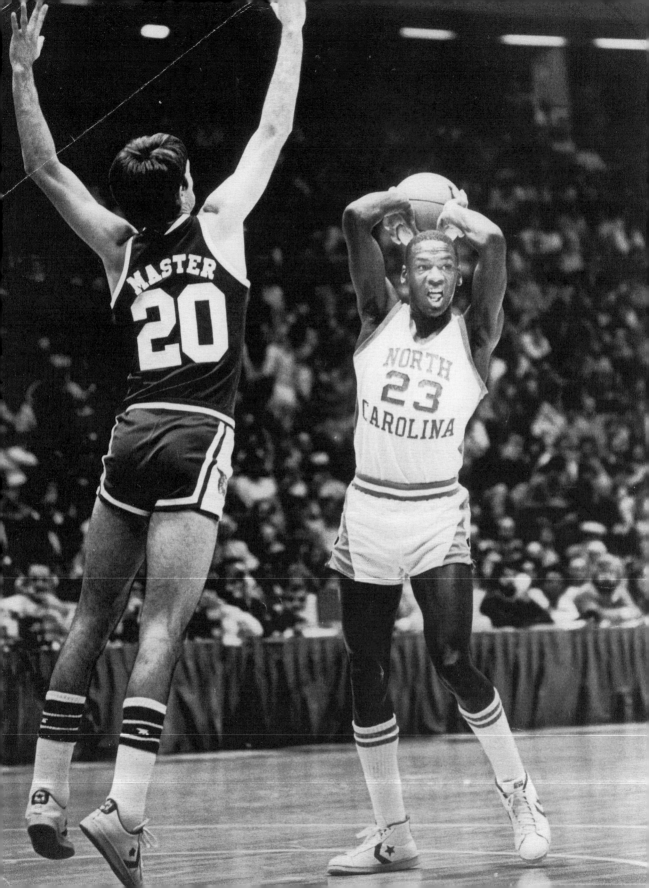

3

ON DEAN'S LIST

Despite his success at Laney High School, Jordan was not regarded as a prize recruit by those colleges with the best basketball programs. Amazingly, he was not even regarded as one of the best basketball players in his home state of North Carolina, let alone in the entire United States.

Most colleges begin targeting their "blue-chip" recruits when those players are just sophomores or juniors in high school, but even as a senior Jordan failed to make a list of the 300 top high-school basketball players in the country. Although he was interested in playing for such basketball powerhouses as the University of Virginia and UCLA, those schools were not interested in him. His counselors at Laney suggested that he forget about playing big-time college basketball and attend a military academy or a Division III school instead. (Division III

Jordan was voted the cockiest freshman by his University of North Carolina teammates, but his performances on court justified his self-confidence.

schools play at the lowest level of college athletics and do not award athletic scholarships.)

Players whose abilities have not yet fully emerged by the time they are sophomores or juniors in high school get overlooked in the college recruiting sweepstakes. If a powerful college basketball team still has any scholarships left over after its top choices commit to its program, maybe—just maybe—they'll save a spot for a potential late-bloomer.

Fortunately for Jordan, the one school seriously interested in him consistently fielded one of the nation's best teams. The University of North Carolina (UNC), coached by the legendary Dean Smith, was always ranked among the nation's 20 top teams, and the Tar Heels, as the UNC athletic teams were known, almost always contended for the national championship.

While other schools were overlooking Jordan, Smith had been tipped off about the Wilmington star's abilities by Roy Williams, his assistant coach, who had seen Jordan play at a basketball camp in the summer before his senior year at Laney. Wanting to see how Jordan would do against topflight competition, Williams asked the famous Five Star basketball camp in Pittsburgh, Pennsylvania, to invite the kid to their sessions.

Five Star was always attended by the nation's best high-school players. An invitation there was proof that a player was one of the country's elite schoolboy hoopsters, and college coaches and recruiters flocked there each summer to evaluate talent. According to Brendan Malone, then an official at Five Star and later an assistant coach with several NBA teams, Jordan had not been invited because "the only people who knew about him were in North Carolina" and "no one was recruiting him at that time." Even after Roy Williams intervened, Jordan was not invited to the first of the camp's three week-long sessions, which was reserved exclusively for those players regarded as the nation's very best.

But once he arrived, Jordan made people pay attention to him, and scouts and recruiters left shaking their heads, wondering how in the world anyone could have overlooked the thin, graceful, acrobatic, explosive 6'3" young man from Wilmington. The player no one seemed to know about could not be stopped by anyone at the camp, no matter how much bigger they were in size or reputation.

"He just steps out on the court and it's like he's playing a different game. It was like there were no defenders," a camp official said at the time. Jordan either went around or jumped over anyone who tried to guard him. Brendan Malone said that "his ability to put the ball on the floor and take it to the hoop really jumped out at you." Jordan was voted the most valuable player award for each of the two sessions he attended. The award made the pleased youngster recognize, perhaps for the first time, the true dimensions of his basketball potential. "It was as though somebody had tapped me on the shoulder with a magic wand and said, 'You must emerge as somebody—somebody to be admired, to achieve great things,'" Jordan remembered some years later.

That emergence was evident the first time he set foot on the University of North Carolina campus in the fall of 1981. Unlike most of UNC's recruits, Jordan did not arrive with a big reputation, but he quickly made a name for himself. A fellow student, Ken Stewart, saw him playing in a pick-up game behind his dormitory. "He came out doing 360s, alley-oops, slamming over people, and that was the first we had heard of him," Stewart recalled.

That "calling attention to himself" sometimes took the form of boasting and taunts—trash-talking, in short. For Jordan, trash-talking marked both the hurt he felt at having his abilities overlooked and a certain lingering insecurity about his abilities. Even after he accepted the scholarship to UNC, people in his hometown told him he should go somewhere else to college, that at a school with so many good players all he would do was sit on the bench. Jordan later confessed that when he started at UNC, "I thought everybody was a superstar and I would be the low man."

Those doubts lasted only as long as his first game as a Tar Heel. In Jordan's first week of practice, Coach Smith learned to his amazement "that we didn't have anyone who could guard him." Soon afterward, Jordan was named to the team's starting five, a rare accomplishment for a freshman. "After the first game," Jordan said, "I realized I was as good as everybody else." In that contest he scored 22 points on superb 11 for 15 shooting from the floor, and he only seemed to get better after that.

"You could see him becoming more sure of himself in everything he did," his teammate James Worthy, an All-American forward, said. "Each game he gained a little respect." While Jordan's physical gifts were readily apparent, it was his on-court intelligence that really impressed Worthy, who told a reporter: "I've never seen anybody pick up the game so fast. Michael just doesn't make mistakes."

Jimmy Black, the team's point guard, was equally impressed by how quickly the team's star freshman adapted to the college game. "Michael can do it all: score, play defense, lead the team, rebound, block shots," Black said. "What else is there?" The coaches in the Atlantic Coast Conference (ACC), where UNC played, agreed with Black's assessment. At season's end, they voted Jordan the league's freshman player of the year.

With Jordan adding his superlative talents to those of Worthy, Black, forward Matt Doherty, and star center Sam Perkins, the Tar Heels easily won the ACC regular-season title and tournament championship. Then it was on to the NCAA tournament, where UNC had often faltered.

For Coach Smith, the NCAA tournament, which determines the national collegiate championship, represented his greatest challenge. Though Smith would eventually win more games than any college coach in history, in his 24 years at North Carolina he had never won a national championship. Smith's critics often pointed to all the superb players he had coached at UNC and shook their heads over his failure to win a national title.

But in the spring of 1982, the talented Tar Heels moved easily through the tournament's opening rounds to the finals, to be played in the Superdome in New Orleans, Louisiana, where they were matched up with Georgetown University. The Hoyas were led by a star freshman of their own, center Patrick Ewing, who was making the first of his three appearances in the finals.

The championship game was an extremely hard fought, nip-and-tuck contest right from the opening tipoff. With 32 seconds remaining, North Carolina, trailing by 1 point, called for a time-out. The obvious play was to work the ball inside to Perkins or the sizzling Worthy, who had already scorched the celebrated Georgetown defense for 28 points.

But Smith knew that Georgetown, with the fearsome Ewing patrolling the lane, would prepare for such a strategy. Instead, he decided—as Jordan's coaches would do so often in the years to come—to put the ball, and the game, in Jordan's hands. The final play was designed for Jordan to take the last shot. "Do it, Michael, just knock it in," the legendary coach whispered to the freshman as the teams returned to the floor.

With the game's last half-minute ticking away, the Tar Heels worked the ball passively around the perimeter. Finally, with about 19 seconds left on the clock, Jimmy Black, on the right side of the court, drew the Georgetown defenders toward him with a quick feint toward the basket and then snapped the ball all the way across the court to Jordan on the left wing.

Jordan caught the ball and went up in the same motion. His jump shot, at this stage in his career the weakest part of his game, tended normally to be flat, without much arc, but this time he unleashed what he later described as "a rainbow."

In the stands of the Superdome, James Jordan covered his face with his hands as his son released the shot. Next to him, Deloris Jordan screamed in delight as the ball swished through the net, giving Carolina the lead. Georgetown

had enough time to get a final shot off, but they rushed the ball upcourt and turned it over to North Carolina. Seconds later, the clock ran out, and the Tar Heels were the national champions.

"That's when everything started," Jordan would say later about what Tar Heel fans always refer to simply as "the shot." "That's when Michael Jordan started to get his respect."

"The Shot"—as Georgetown's Eric Smith looks on and Patrick Ewing hopes for a rebound, Michael Jordan releases the jumper that won the 1982 NCAA championship.

4
RED, WHITE, AND BLUE

When Jordan began his sophomore season in the fall of 1982, Coach Smith felt that he had improved in virtually every aspect of his game: "defense, confidence, rebounding, position, passing, ball handling." Jordan had spent seemingly every spare moment of the past six months in Woollen Gymnasium on the UNC campus, playing in pick-up games with past and present Tar Heels and dominating every contest. The difference between Jordan as a freshman and Jordan as a sophomore, Smith felt, was "like night and day."

An improved Jordan was a frightening prospect for his opponents, but the Tar Heels were not as strong a team as the previous year. Worthy had moved on to the pros, and a couple of newcomers, center Brad Daugherty and guard Kenny Smith, were not ready to pick up the slack. Though UNC tied for the ACC regular-season title, they lost in the early rounds of

In 1984, Jordan was named Player of the Year by both his conference and United Press International.

both the conference and NCAA tournaments.

The superlatives poured in for Jordan's play, however. A local reporter called him the "best all around player in college basketball" and the "most talented player North Carolina or the ACC has ever seen." The *Sporting News* agreed with the first part of that assessment and named Jordan their college player of the year. *Sports Illustrated*'s college basketball maven, Curry Kirkpatrick, proclaimed Jordan to be "merely the finest all-around amateur player in the world." Jeff Mullins, a former ACC player and star in the NBA, believed that once Jordan turned pro, he would make it necessary for experts to revise their opinion that Jerry West and Oscar Robertson were the two greatest guards of all time.

Hopes were high, therefore, as UNC approached its 1983-84 season. The Tar Heels boasted college basketball's best player, as well as multi-talented big man Sam Perkins, an All-American; Smith and Daugherty also were ready to play major roles. Virtually every preseason poll had North Carolina ranked number one in the nation.

With Jordan playing the most well-rounded ball of his career and compiling a conference-leading 19.6 point average per game while shooting an excellent 55 percent from the floor, Carolina swept through the regular season. The Tar Heels did not lose a game in the conference and only one overall, and that by just one point, and they maintained their number one ranking for most of the season.

But once again UNC faltered in the tournament, losing to inferior squads in the semifinals of the ACC tournament and the regional semifinals of the NCAA tournament.

For Jordan, who once again won several college player of the year awards, the tournament losses marked a bitter end to his career at North Carolina. On May 5, 1984, with the blessing of his father and Coach Smith, he announced that he would forgo his senior year at UNC to enter the professional ranks.

There was still one more challenge left for him as an amateur player, however. In the early summer of 1984, Jordan tried out for the basketball team that would represent the United States later that year at the Olympic Games in Los Angeles, California.

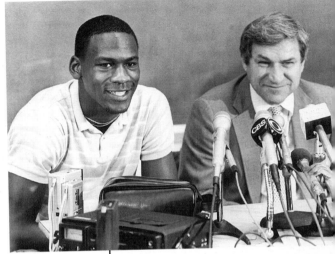

His mother protested, but his father and Coach Dean Smith (right) approved when Michael Jordan announced that he would skip his senior year and turn pro.

Many observers wondered how Jordan would fare with the Olympic squad, for the team's coach was Bobby Knight of Indiana University, generally regarded as the hardest driving, most demanding coach in the game, and an absolute stickler for fundamentals. Though Jordan possessed a supreme understanding of the game, his talent is so immense and so individual that he often succeeded in ways that are not, from a coach's standpoint, strictly fundamentally "correct."

For example, players are always schooled never to "leave their feet"—to jump in the air—with the ball without knowing for certain if they are going to shoot or pass, and if the latter, to whom. Justifiably confident in his leaping and ability to improvise a solution, Jordan consistently violated this rule. "If I thought about a move, I'd probably turn the ball over," he has said. "I just look at a situation in the air, adjust, create, and let instinct take over."

For some coaches, such an approach can be a dilemma. Phil Jackson, the best of Jordan's coaches in the professional ranks, explained: "Michael Jordan is a coach's dream and a coach's nightmare at the same time. He knows that there are ways for him to short-cut things and beat the system. So for every incredible thing he does, he does something that defies the rules of the game. Like when the double team comes at him, instead of passing the ball, he beats the double team."

Many people predicted that such an approach would never fly with Knight, and they predicted clashes between the volatile coach and the confident young superstar. After all, hadn't Knight cut from the Olympic team another freewheeling superstar, a forward from Auburn University named Charles Barkley, after taking a dislike to his flamboyant, unorthodox game? And many observers felt that Barkley had been the best player in the Olympic try-out camps.

But to the surprise of some, Knight was quick to understand that to insist that Jordan do everything by the book, exactly the way lesser players were drilled to play, would be to stifle the creativity that allowed him to do so many

In 1983, Jordan led the U.S. basketball team to a gold medal at the Pan-American Games. The following year he and his teammates won the gold at the Olympic Games.

things that others could not. It would likely hamper him as much as insisting that he abandon his childlike habit of leaving his tongue dangling from his open mouth as he moved otherwise so gracefully about the hardwood.

Knight, the harshest coaching taskmaster of them all, took a lenient approach with Jordan. "The first few times he did that [leaving his feet with the ball] in practice," remembered C. M. Newton, one of Knight's assistant coaches with the Olympic team, "Coach Knight would stop practice and explain to him why it was wrong. But then we noticed that he could hang in the air for so long and do so many things with the ball that he was almost always successful. So we stopped coaching him after that."

With Jordan leading the way, assisted by such other future professional stars as Chris Mullin and Patrick Ewing, the U. S. team went virtually unchallenged as it swept its way to the gold medal by an average margin of victory of 32 points a game. Jordan, says Bobby Knight to this day, is simply the best player he has ever worked with.

Jordan's Olympic opponents had a more visceral response to his enormous talents, one summed up by Fernando Martin of Spain's team and that would soon be impressed upon his NBA opponents as well. "Michael Jordan?" said Martin in response to a reporter's question. "Jump, jump, jump. Very quick. Very fast. Jump, jump, jump."

5

AIR JORDAN

For all his collegiate brilliance, Jordan was only the third player in the 1984 NBA draft. The Houston Rockets used their first pick to select Hakeem Olajuwon and the Portland Trailblazers next chose Sam Bowie. Both played center, and conventional basketball wisdom held that a big man was the necessary first building block of a championship team.

Hard as it is now to believe, many people did not expect that Jordan would be a superstar in professional basketball. Despite the steady brilliance of his play at UNC, Jordan's star had never been allowed to shine as brightly as it might have. In part, this was because the college game, with its zone defenses, slower pace, and different style of officiating, placed less of an emphasis on quickness and the ability to put the ball on the floor and break down an individual defender with the dribble than did the profes-

Michael Jordan was an instant hit in the NBA—with the fans. Other players, such as Steve Stipanovich (left) and Kenton Edelin (right) of the Indiana Pacers, tried to contain the explosive rookie.

sional game, and these were precisely the areas in which Jordan most excelled.

In addition, Coach Smith's offense emphasized passing, moving without the ball, picks and screens. Players were told to shoot only when the structure of the offense created scoring opportunities. They were not supposed to create individually, which was more Jordan's style.

The result, according to Brendan Malone, was that at the time of the NBA draft, "nobody, I don't care who they are, thought he would develop into a superstar. Everybody thought he'd be a good player, a very good player in [the NBA], but not to the point where you'd say he's the best one-on-one player who ever played the game."

It took the Chicago Bulls just a few scrimmage games in training camp in the autumn of 1984 to recognize Jordan's talent. "If I put him with the starters, they win," raved Chicago's coach, Kevin Loughery. "If I put him with the second team, they win. If I put him on the offensive team, it seems his team always scores. When I put him on the defensive team, they always stop the offensive team. No matter what I do with Michael, his team wins."

Shellshocked players and coaches around the league were soon echoing similar sentiments. T. R. Dunn of the Denver Nuggets, one of the league's best defensive guards, discerned no weaknesses in Jordan's game: "He can shoot, penetrate, pass, handle the ball and, whew, everyone knows he can jump."

For several seasons, the Bulls had resided near the bottom of the NBA standings. As word of Jordan's aerial displays spread, they found themselves playing before sell-out crowds virtually everywhere they went. With Jordan's commercials for his new Nike sneakers—Air Jordans—playing on network television across the country, the highflying rookie was treated to exhibitions of fan and media interest usually reserved for touring rock stars.

For one observer, all the attention given Jordan was well deserved. Larry Bird was then in the midst of the second of his three straight MVP seasons and was by general acclaim the NBA's best all-around player. Yet after his Celtics played Jordan's Bulls for the first time, Bird, who was customarily not generous with praise, stated that Jordan (who had tallied 41 points, 12 rebounds, and 7 assists) was "the best. Never seen anyone like him. Unlike anyone I've ever seen. Phenomenal. One of a kind. He's the best. Ever." And that included himself, the proud Bird added.

But for all his immediate greatness, Jordan could not singlehandedly pull the Bulls above mediocrity. Although the sensational rookie led his team in scoring (more than 28 points per game), rebounding (more than 6 per game, despite playing guard), and assists (almost 6 per game)—a feat accomplished by just two other players in NBA history, Dave Cowens and the hallowed Bird—the Bulls, a talented but troubled bunch, won just 38 of their 82 games. Still, that was enough to qualify them for the NBA playoffs, though they were easily eliminated in the first round.

Despite his personal success and popularity, Jordan, who made the All-Star team and was the nearly unanimous choice for rookie of the year, was not satisfied with his season. Losing frustrated him, as did the lack of dedication and drive

Orlando Woolridge (right), shown here working out against Michael Jordan, once said that traveling with the phenomenally popular Jordan was like "touring with Michael Jackson."

in many of his teammates. Several of the Bulls had problems with substance abuse, and many of the others seemed more concerned with playing time and salary than they did with winning.

Jordan's frustrations increased during the 1985-86 season. Chicago had fired Coach Loughery, whom he liked, and replaced him with Stan Albeck. The Bulls' roster was essentially the same as the previous season, and when Chicago dropped all eight of its preseason games, Jordan began what would become a pattern of berating the Bulls' front office for its failure to upgrade the on-court talent.

Disaster struck in just the third game of the season, when Jordan broke a small bone in his left foot while running upcourt. Up until that point, he had never missed a game in his high-school, college, or professional career, but he would be forced to sit out 63 contests while waiting for the bone to heal. Frustrated, Jordan quarreled with his doctors, criticized his team-mates publicly, and argued with Chicago management when they suggested he sit out the rest of the year instead of trying to return.

Ignoring his doctors' and Chicago management's recommendation, Jordan returned to the floor on March 15, 1986, near the end of the regular season. His return allowed the Bulls to sneak into the playoffs and set the stage for one of the most incredible performances in NBA history. In the first game of the opening round of the playoffs, against the Boston Celtics, Jordan lit up his defender, premier guard Dennis Johnson, for an astounding 49 points.

But game one was just a warm-up. In the second contest, Jordan scored an astounding 63 points, going over and around a host of bewildered Boston defenders. In the game's most memorable sequence, soon to be a staple of league highlight films, he went one-on-one with Bird when the Celtic forward jumped out on a switch to guard him deep in the right corner. Juking in several different directions while dribbling the ball rapidly back and forth between his legs, Jordan created an illusion of motion that sent Bird scurrying backward, then embarked on a tortuous foray along the baseline that took him around Johnson, who had rushed to the overmatched Bird's aid. Met then by Kevin McHale, Jordan took to the air, elevating above and beyond the reach of him and the late-arriving Boston center, Robert Parish, to emerge on the far side of the basket, where he flipped the ball off glass and through the hoop.

"I think he's God disguised as Michael Jordan," a relieved Bird said afterward, his mood lightened by the Celtics' win in double overtime. "He is the most awesome player in the NBA."

6

THE JORDAN RULES

Bird's comments marked what would threaten to become a disturbing pattern in Jordan's career: unprecedented personal recognition and achievement combined with a lack of team success. For all his brilliance, the Bulls lost their playoff series in three straight games to the Celtics. Over the next several seasons, Jordan would rise to all manner of individual heights, only to be disappointed by the Bulls' collective failure to achieve at the same level.

Jordan followed up his performance in the 1986 playoffs with a one-man assault on the record books that lasted the course of the entire season. When he was through, he had not only won the first of what would be a record-tying seven consecutive scoring titles, but had scored at a higher rate than any guard in NBA history—an astounding 37.1 points per game.

In winning the slam dunk contest at the 1988 All-Star Game, Jordan revealed how a dunk could combine grace, power, and creativity.

The season was a cavalcade of personal highlights. Jordan scored 50 or more points in a game nine separate times. He scored 61 points in a game twice. During one streak, he scored 40 or more points in nine consecutive contests. In the season opener, he served notice of things to come by scoring 50 points against the New York Knicks. Three weeks later, against the same opponent, he scored his team's final 18 points, including the game-winning jump shot with eight seconds left to play. Later in the season, he set an NBA record by scoring 23 consecutive points against the Atlanta Hawks. When Philadelphia 76er Charles Barkley threatened to "break him up in little pieces" to keep his scoring in check, Jordan notched 47. In his last-ever match-up with the legendary Julius Erving, he scored 56, on a night when the Bulls as a team only managed 93.

In addition to his scoring feats, Jordan became the first player in NBA history to record more than 100 blocked shots and 200 steals in the same season. He received more votes than any other player for the All-Star game, and he won the annual mid-season slam dunk contest. His popularity with fans seemed to know no bounds, and he became, clearly, the most admired and emulated athlete in America. To make matters complete, he met Juanita Vanoy, a bank officer, who would become his wife and the mother of his three children.

But for Jordan, the accolades all had a certain hollowness to them, for the Bulls were still not a very good team. In 1986-87, they won just 40 of their 82 games and were again eliminated in the first round of the playoffs.

Basketball mavens were quick to acknowledge that Jordan was by far the game's most talented and spectacular talent. But Larry Bird and Magic Johnson were considered the best players. Bird's Celtics had won three NBA championships in his time with the club, and lost twice more in the finals. Before Magic's playing career was ended, his Lakers would tally five championships and nine trips to the finals.

With their superlative passing skills, Bird and Johnson made their teammates better, it was argued, resulting in their team's ultimate success; Jordan's one-on-one style rewarded only himself. His critics were also quick to point out that no player had ever led the league in scoring and played on a championship team in the same season.

The criticism clearly irked Jordan. Before the 1987-88 season began, he gave an interview in which he unfavorably but correctly rated the talent of his own teammates. The Boston and Los Angeles greats, Jordan rightly pointed out, were surrounded by All-Stars; anybody who did not think that it was easier for Johnson and Bird to make their teammates better was a "damn fool," Jordan said.

In many ways, Jordan's 1987-88 season was even better than the record-breaking one that preceded it. Though his scoring average declined two points, to a still spectacular 35 points per game, his shooting percentage was up, from a fine 48 percent to an absolutely superb 54 percent. His rebounds and assists totals also increased. Observers thought his game was steadier, more well-rounded, and he was voted the first of the three Most Valuable Player awards he would win. For the first time as well, his defensive prowess was recognized, as he was voted the league's defensive player of the year. Jordan remains the only player in NBA history to win a scoring championship, MVP award, and defensive player of the year award in the course of a career, let alone in a single season. In fact, no other player has even won a scoring championship and a defensive player of the year award, or an MVP with a defensive player of the year award.

At long last, the Bulls, with the addition of rookies Horace Grant and Scottie Pippen and the continued strong rebounding of forward Charles Oakley, were a much improved team. Under coach Doug Collins, who had replaced Albeck in the fall of 1986, Chicago won 50 games and for the first time in Jordan's career advanced beyond the first round of the playoffs, defeating the Cleveland Cavaliers, with Jordan averaging an otherworldly 45 points a game.

But then, in what would become a disturbing springtime ritual for Chicago, the Bulls were ousted from the playoffs by their most hated rivals. For the next two seasons, the trend would continue: Jordan would lead the league in scoring and aerial acrobatics, play his customary airtight defense, and lead the ever-improving Bulls to a fine regular-season record, including a superb 55 wins in 1989-90, and victory in the first two rounds of the playoffs. Then the Bulls would run up against the Detroit Pistons.

The bad blood between the two teams went back to Jordan's rookie year, when Detroit's star guard, Isiah Thomas, organized a "freeze-out" of Jordan in that season's All-Star Game. Thomas, like several other established NBA stars, was jealous of Jordan's immediate popularity and unprecedented success with commercial endorsements, and he supposedly convinced several of

his and Jordan's teammates on the All-Star team not to pass the ball to the Chicago rookie. The two superstars had feuded ever since; in 1992, Jordan even supposedly made it a condition of his participation on the U.S. Olympic team—the so-called Dream Team—that Thomas not be named to the squad.

In addition, Detroit had become one of the elite teams in the NBA by perfecting an especially rugged, unyielding, physical style of play. Other players called the Pistons thugs, but the Detroit players reveled in their image as the league's "Bad Boys." Detroit was admittedly the league's best defensive five, but other teams, especially the Bulls, felt that they consistently and intentionally crossed the fine line that separates physical and aggressive from dirty and dangerous play. The Pistons clutched and grabbed, they held, they elbowed, they undercut, and when they fouled, they fouled hard, hoping thereby to intimidate opponents or at least sap their determination. Their aim was to slow the pace of each game to a virtual crawl, to turn each game into the professional-basketball equivalent of a street fight.

Michael Jordan looks on as Scottie Pippen sails in for a layup over Houston's Purvis Short. Pippen's arrival immediately made the Bulls a better team, but it took them a few years before they could get past the first round of the playoffs.

48

MICHAEL JORDAN

Such a style was especially frustrating to the Bulls, who, with Jordan and Pippen, flourished when the premium was on quickness and finesse. With some degree of justification, Jordan felt that Detroit players had several times intentionally tried to injure him, and over the years the teams had engaged in a number of memorable oncourt brawls after Jordan was flagrantly fouled. Still, year in and year out, the Pistons dominated the Bulls, finishing ahead of them in the Central Division during the regular season and ousting them from the conference semi-finals in 1988 and from the conference finals in 1989 and 1990. Detroit's dominance of Chicago was made possible by a set of defensive strategies known as the Jordan Rules. In their essence, the Jordan Rules were simple: All five defensive players had to be aware of where Jordan was at all times, and he was to be double-teamed every time he touched the ball.

Isiah Thomas (left) and Joe Dumars ran over Michael Jordan and the Bulls in the 1990 playoffs.

The Pistons counted on the fact that Jordan's teammates were accustomed to him dominating the offense and taking every important shot and would thus fail to "step up" and take some of the pressure off of him, particularly in crucial playoff contests.

Veteran NBA observers, not to mention Jordan, noted that the Pistons also practiced an unwritten corollary to the Jordan Rules. To Frank Layden, then the coach of the Utah Jazz, all the talk about the mysterious Jordan Rules ignored their extremely simple essence. "You know what the Jordan rule is, don't you?" Layden said. "Knock him on his ass. Detroit can talk all they want, but the one thing they did—when he got in midair—they knocked him down."

As executed by Detroit's superior defensive personnel, the Jordan Rules consistently frustrated the Chicago star and his teammates. Although Jordan still scored against the Pistons at a high rate, Detroit made him work extremely hard for his points. Forced to shoulder a greater share of the scoring burden than under usual circumstances, Jordan's teammates usually wilted under Detroit's pressure and tactics of intimidation.

Still, virtually singlehanded, Jordan was able to extend the Pistons to a seventh game in both the 1989 and 1990 playoffs; in each of those years his teammates failed to give him the support he needed in the crucial contest, and the Bulls went down to defeat. Detroit, meanwhile, went on to claim the NBA championship that Jordan craved so desperately, with neither of their opponents in the finals giving them as much opposition as had the Bulls.

For Jordan, the most galling defeat took place in the spring of 1990. Chicago's 55 wins in the just-concluded regular season had given the Bulls the second-best record in the league. Even though the best record belonged to the hated Pistons, the Bulls and their fans were confident that this would be the year Chicago would eliminate Detroit in the playoffs and move on to the championship round.

Jordan had put in his typically stellar regular season, leading the league in scoring for the fourth consecutive year, making the All-NBA first team for the fourth of seven consecutive years, making the NBA All-Defense first team for the third of six consecutive years, and playing what he would describe as his "greatest game," a career-high performance against the Cleveland Cavaliers in which he tallied 69 points and 18 rebounds. He had then prepared for the showdown with Detroit by playing what he described as the best four consecutive games of his life—averaging 43 points, 7 rebounds, and 7 assists—in the course of Chicago's five-game playoff win over the Philadelphia 76ers.

His teammates, too, seemed better prepared for Detroit. Center Bill Cartwright had replaced Oakley, giving the Bulls the proven low-post scorer they had always lacked in Jordan's time with the club. After three years in the league, Pippen was blossoming into a remarkable player, a Jordanesque combination of height, quickness, speed, explosive leaping ability, and offensive creativity who complemented Jordan superbly in Chicago's offensive and defensive schemes. Chicago also featured a new head coach: Laid-back but demanding Phil Jackson had replaced Doug Collins, whose manic tirades had alienated most of the players on the team.

After two games of the series, there seemed little reason for Chicago's optimism. The Pistons won both easily, while holding the Bulls to a sickly 77 and 93 points. Jordan averaged 27 points per game (5 points below his regular-season average), on less than 40 percent shooting (as opposed to the 53 percent he shot during the regular season). Slammed repeatedly to the floor by the Bad Boys, he exited game two limping. As always against Detroit, his teammates appeared tentative and confused. His backcourt mates, Craig Hodges and John Paxson, missed all their shots in game one, and Pippen admitted to being intimidated by the flypaper defense of Dennis Rodman. Angry and frustrated, at halftime of game two Jordan threw a chair around the lockerroom and cursed his teammates.

With Jordan averaging more than 40 points a game in the Chicago wins, the Bulls regrouped to take three of the next four contests and set the stage for a deciding game seven. Although Jordan scored or assisted on every Chicago basket of the second half until he left the game, Detroit won easily, 93-74. As had happened in previous years, Jordan's fellow Bulls "disappeared" at the critical moments. Pleading the excuse of a migraine, Pippen shot just 1 for 10 from the floor. Grant was little better, at 3 for 17. B. J. Armstrong was 1 for 8, and Craig Hodges was 3 for 13. For the series, Jordan shot 47 percent from the floor—below average for him, but exceptional against Detroit's superb defense—while his teammates managed only an atrocious 38 percent. "We have to do some things. We have to make some changes," a grim Jordan said in the mournful Chicago lockerroom afterwards.

Coach Phil Jackson's unusual motivational techniques—he once spliced shots of Sioux warrior purification ceremonies into Chicago game films—helped raise the Bulls' level of play.

7

THOSE CHAMPIONSHIP SEASONS

To Jordan's great disappointment, the team did not make any significant changes in personnel prior to the beginning of the 1990-91 season. To him, the fulfillment of his dream of a championship thus seemed farther away than ever. Tiring of the relentless scrutiny that his fame occasioned—Jordan found it impossible to even enjoy such simple pleasures as eating out in a restaurant without being mobbed—he began to speak of retirement and warned "that people may have already seen the best of me." Basketball, he said, was for him now "like a business."

The season did not begin well for the Bulls. Jordan was suspicious of a new offensive system installed by Jackson to allow all of the Bulls to participate more fully in the Chicago offense. Though he agreed to give the so-called triangle offense a chance, Jordan warned "that if things start going wrong, I'm going to start shooting."

Jordan will always be remembered as a winner. His joy, displayed here after the 1992 victory over the Portland Trailblazers, was contagious.

When the Bulls front office ignored Jordan's suggestion that it obtain guard Walter Davis, a longtime NBA star who was available, Jordan resumed his perennial quarrel with general manager Jerry Krause. With the current roster, Jordan insisted, Chicago was simply not good enough to win the title.

In past years, Jordan had made the same charge—and had been correct. Now, though Chicago's roster was unchanged, the players themselves were different. The nucleus of the team had now played together for several years, and they had learned how to complement each other's skills.

Cartwright, whose skills Jordan had initially disdained, slowly won over his teammate with his ungainly but effective game. The youngest starters, Pippen and Grant, continued to mature as players. At Jordan's prodding, Chicago finally settled on steady but unspectacular John Paxson as his backcourt mate. A superb jump shooter when set up by a pass from a teammate, Paxson proved to be the perfect complement to the more creative Jordan.

Coach Jackson also made a huge difference. He recognized that there was still one weapon in Jordan's formidable arsenal that had not been fully utilized: his defense. In fact, with Jordan, Pippen, and Grant, Chicago possessed three players with the skills to guard players of virtually any size the entire length of the court. All were phenomenally quick, with long arms, great leaping ability, rare gifts of anticipation, and the speed to double-team and press in the backcourt and still get back to pick up their assigned man. Assistant coach John Bach called the trio "the Dobermans," and Jackson unleashed them.

Soon, Chicago was devastating opponents with a series of traps and presses that led to myriad turnovers, fast breaks, and easy baskets that led to even easier wins, and they became a team as feared for its defense as the dreaded Pistons.

Jordan had often been aloof and critical of his teammates, but as the team jelled and continually improved, he exhibited an increased confidence in them. He grew especially close to the sometimes unfocused Pippen, whose game flourished as he began to emulate Jordan's relentless approach, giving Chicago a two-pronged attack that no team in the league could match. With Jordan winning his fifth straight scoring title and second MVP award, the Bulls swept through the regular season, winning 61 games to finish on top of the Central Division. They then steamrolled through the first two rounds of the playoffs, losing only one game to advance to the conference finals and a fourth straight postseason rendezvous with the Pistons.

For the Bulls and their long-disappointed fans, the series proved anticlimactic in its easiness. Shockingly, the Bulls disposed of their nemesis in four straight games, dominating every contest by emulating Detroit's bullying tactics. "They stole our playbook," said Detroit's John Salley afterwards. "Talking junk, talking garbage, making sure there is only one shot, keeping people out of the middle, making people beat them with their jump shot. That's what we usually do." Unable to bear the turnabout, Isiah Thomas led his teammates off the floor with a few seconds still remaining in the final game so that they would not have to congratulate the victors.

Chicago's victory set up a dream matchup in the NBA finals with the Los Angeles Lakers, who

The "Dream Team" has been called the greatest team ever to play in any sport. Jordan flashes the victory sign, along with Scottie Pippen and Clyde Drexler.

in Magic Johnson's twelfth year with the club were making a remarkable ninth appearance in the final round of the playoffs. Again, however, on the court the showdown proved to be a mismatch. After losing the opening game on a last-second shot, the Bulls handily won four straight contests to claim the NBA crown. With Magic handcuffed by Pippen's remarkable defense, Jordan dominated him in every phase of the game, even amassing more assists than Johnson, who was generally acclaimed as the greatest passer of the era. With back ailments forcing Bird ever closer into retirement, there now seemed to be no doubt about who was the best all-around player in the game. In the jubilant Chicago locker room after the final game of the series, Jordan clutched the gold championship trophy as if he would never let it go and broke down in huge sobs.

Jordan's supremacy was made even clearer in the 1991-92 season. Chicago romped through the regular season with an absolutely superb total of 67 wins. Jordan notched his sixth straight scoring championship and second straight MVP award. Though the New York Knicks surprisingly extended the Bulls in the conference semifinals by emulating Detroit's roughhouse style, Chicago was no longer intimidated by such tactics, and they easily whipped the Knicks in the series' seventh game and went on to oust the Cleveland Cavaliers to set up a second straight appearance in the finals.

Their opponent this time was the Portland Trailblazers, led by shooting guard Clyde Drexler. Some NBA observers had suggested that Drexler, who played an athletic, high-flying game similar to Jordan's, was the Chicago stalwart's equal as an all-around player. But Jordan's superiority was made frighteningly apparent in just the first-half of the first game of the Championship Series, when he scorched Drexler for an NBA record six three-point field goals en route to another record 35 points.

The badly shaken Drexler never recovered; he spent the rest of the series chasing Jordan and forcing ill-conceived shots, and Portland actually played better when he was off the floor. It took Chicago six games to win its second-straight title. Jordan's thorough dominance of the league's second-best player was simply astonishing; never had the gap between himself and his peers been made so manifestly clear.

That dominance was exhibited again in the summer of 1992, when Jordan was the brightest of the NBA stars who made up the U.S. "Dream Team" that won the gold medal in basketball at the Summer Olympic Games in Barcelona, Spain. The U.S. squad so outclassed its opponents that its most significant competition took place in practice.

Only off the court did Jordan seem vulnerable. The number of his commercial endorsements had risen, to the point where he was by far the most successful athletic pitchman in history, yet his image had been tarnished by a number of events. A book called *The Jordan Rules*, by Chicago sportswriter Sam Smith, portrayed him as relentlessly competitive and driven. He was criticized for the extremely high price of his Air Jordan sneakers, which his immense popularity had made a status symbol among poor black children in the inner cities—precisely those who were least able to afford them. Most damaging of all were reports, based on the discovery of cancelled checks in the automobile trunk of a murdered drug dealer, that he frequently gambled for extremely high stakes, often with unsavory characters.

The endless scrutiny to which his on and off-court life was now subjected caused Jordan to contemplate retirement again. His father, who throughout Jordan's career had remained his most trusted and closest advisor, had suggested he give up the game after Chicago's first championship, but Jordan decided that there was still one goal for him to reach.

He therefore took the floor for the 1992-93 season to compete not so much against the rest of the league as against history and the ghosts of two recently retired players—Magic Johnson and Larry Bird. Jordan's goal was to accomplish something neither of them had managed to do: win three straight NBA championships.

Jordan casually claimed his record-tying seventh straight scoring crown. The Bulls posted only the league's third-best regular-season record, but they regrouped in the playoffs. With Jordan playing at a phenomenal level, even for him, they rallied past the New York Knicks to advance to the NBA finals against the Phoenix Suns and forward Charles Barkley, who had wrested Jordan's MVP trophy away from him in the regular season. But in the championship round, Jordan again demonstrated that there could be no reasonable debate about who the league's best player was, as he averaged an unprecedented 41 points per game—a record for the championship round—and led Chicago to a six-game victory. The Bulls thus became the first NBA team to win three straight championships in almost 30 years.

As the inevitable postseason discussions centered on whether Chicago's feat qualified the team as one of the greatest ever, surprisingly little debate could be heard as to whether Jordan could now be considered, without reservation, the greatest player in history. The matter, all concerned seemingly agreed, had been convincingly settled once and for all.

Certainly, in Jordan's mind there was no question. Just several days before the Bulls were to begin training camp in October 1993, Jordan stunned the world—his fame was indeed that immense—by announcing his retirement from the game. Speculation as to his reasons immediately focused on the death of his beloved father, who had been brutally murdered that past summer, and on the continued investigations into his gambling. But, said Jordan, the reason for his sudden departure was much simpler. There were no more challenges for him on the court, and he had always planned to go out on top. He had, he said, nothing left to prove.

It was hard to argue with that statement. What he had demonstrated in 12 years of basketball at the collegiate and professional levels (three at UNC, nine with Chicago) was unprecedented and took many lines of the record book to delineate. So Jordan decided to skip the 1993-94 NBA season and spend the spring and summer of 1994 playing the outfield in the Chicago White Sox' baseball organization.

Jordan's baseball career ended as quickly as it began. A strike put an early halt to the 1994 season and was still not settled when spring training began in 1995. Rather than play with inferior "replacement" players, he returned—with much fanfare—on March 19, 1995 to the Chicago Bulls, who had been struggling all season long.

Jordan tried to lift the Bulls to yet another NBA title. But try as he might, he was unable to get them past the Orlando Magic in the second round of the 1995 playoffs. As Jordan left the court, minus a fourth championship, basketball held a challenge for him once again.

After winning yet another championship, Michael Jordan thanked his best friend: his father.

STATISTICS

MICHAEL JEFFREY JORDAN
(Chicago Bulls)

SEASON	G	MIN	FGM	FGA	PCT	FTM	FTA	PCT	RBD	AST	PTS	AVG
1984-85	82	3144	837	1625	.515	630	746	.845	534	481	**2313**	28.2
1985-86	18	451	150	328	.457	105	125	.840	64	53	408	22.7
1986-87	82	**3281**	**1098**	**2279**	.482	**833**	**972**	.857	430	377	**3041**	**37.1**
1987-88	82	**3311**	**1069**	**1998**	.535	**723**	860	.841	449	485	**2868**	**35.0**
1988-89	81	**3255**	**966**	**1795**	.538	674	793	.850	652	650	**2633**	**32.5**
1989-90	82	**3197**	**1034**	**1964**	.526	593	699	.848	565	519	**2753**	**33.6**
1990-91	82	3034	**990**	**1837**	.539	571	671	.851	492	453	**2580**	**31.5**
1991-92	80	3102	**943**	**1818**	.519	491	590	.832	511	489	**2404**	**30.1**
1994-95	17	668	166	404	.411	109	136	.801	117	90	457	**26.9**
Totals	684	26510	8245	16051	.510	5205	6161	.840	4336	4025	21998	**32.2**
Playoff Totals	120	5021	1518	3040	.500	1002	1228	.820	798	776	4132	34.4
All-Star Totals	8	239	74	150	.493	27	36	.750	31	29	177	22.1

G	games
MIN	minutes
FGA	field goals attempted
FGM	field goals made
PCT	percent
FTA	free throws attempted
FTM	free throws made
RBD	rebounds
AST	assists
PTS	points
AVG	scoring average

bold indicates league-leading figures

Records still held:

highest scoring average, career: 32.3
most consecutive years leading league
   in scoring: 7 (tied)
most points, one playoff game: 63
most consecutive points, one NBA game: 23

MICHAEL JORDAN
A CHRONOLOGY

1963   Michael Jeffrey Jordan born on February 17 in Brooklyn, New York

1978   Cut from the varsity basketball team at Laney High School in Wilmington, NC

1980   Wins MVP award for two sessions at Five Star Camp in Pittsburgh, PA

1982   Scores winning points that give North Carolina Tar Heels the national collegiate championship

1983   Leads U.S. team to gold medal in the Pan-American Games in Venezuela

1984   Drafted by the Chicago Bulls; sparks U.S. team to gold medal in the Summer Olympic Games in Los Angeles

1985   Obtains national endorsements for McDonald's, Coca-Cola, and Nike; leads the Bulls in scoring, rebounding, and assists; wins NBA Rookie of the Year Award

1986   Breaks a bone in his foot; returns to lead Chicago to the playoffs; sets playoff scoring marks against the Boston Celtics

1987   Wins first of seven consecutive scoring championships

1988   Named MVP and Defensive Player of the Year, the first player to win both honors in the same year; scores record 40 points in the NBA All-Star Game

1989   Shoots the winning basket at the buzzer in the deciding playoff game against Cleveland

1991   Wins second MVP award; Chicago wins the NBA championship

1992   Wins third MVP award, second Olympic Gold medal; Chicago wins second straight NBA championship

1993   Wins seventh straight scoring crown; leads league in steals; named to NBA all-defensive team for sixth straight season; wins MVP of championship round for third straight year; Chicago wins third straight NBA championship; announces his retirement

1994   Pursues a career as a professional baseball player

1995   Rejoins the Chicago Bulls

SUGGESTIONS FOR FURTHER READING

Axthelm, Pete. *The City Game: Basketball from the Garden to the Playground.* New York: Penguin, 1982.

Dolan, Sean. *Magic Johnson.* New York: Chelsea House, 1993.

George, Nelson. *Elevating the Game: The History and Aesthetics of Black Men in Basketball.* New York: Simon & Schuster, 1992.

Halberstam, David. *The Breaks of the Game.* New York: Knopf, 1981.

Hollander, Zander, and Alex Sachare. *The Official NBA Basketball Encyclopedia.* New York: New American Library, 1989.

Naughton, Jim. *Taking to the Air.* New York: Warner, 1992.

Sakamoto, Bob. *Michael "Air" Jordan—MVP and NBA Champ.* Lincolnwood, IL: Publications International, 1991.

Smith, Sam. *The Jordan Rules: The Inside Story of a Turbulent Season with Michael Jordan and the Chicago Bulls.* New York: Simon & Schuster, 1992.

Stauth, Cameron. *The Golden Boys: The Unauthorized Inside Look at the U.S. Olympic Basketball Team.* New York: Simon & Schuster, 1992.

Telander, Rick. *Heaven is a Playground.* New York: Simon & Schuster, 1988.

INDEX

ABOUT THE AUTHOR

Sean Dolan has a degree in literature and American history from SUNY Oswego. He is the author of many biographies and histories for young adult readers, including James Beckwourth and Magic Johnson in the BLACK AMERICANS OF ACHIEVEMENT series, and has edited a series of volumes on the famous explorers of history.